**Dilemmas
in Modern
Science**

Health
Ethical debates in
modern medicine

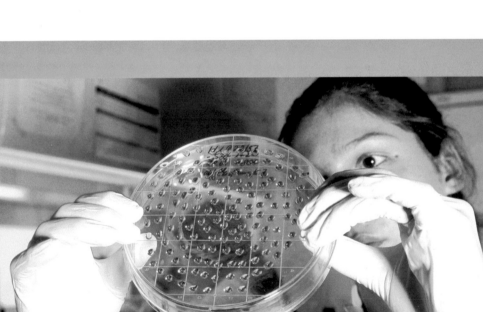

RAY LOVEGROVE

 Contents

● Introduction **6**

Ethical Care **8**

● Drugs and Drug Testing **12**

Organ Transplants **18**

● Genetic Engineering **24**

● Stem-Cell Research **30**

● Modern Medicine and You **36**

Timeline **42**

● Further Information **43**

Glossary **44**

● Index **46**

Introduction

Humans are pushing the boundaries of science and technology. We can access information at the touch of a button. We can genetically modify food so that it grows faster and tastes better. We have developed medicines that can cure once-fatal illnesses. All this might sound positive, but we are now facing many dilemmas in the areas of science, technology and medicine. Just because we *can* do something, does this mean we *should*?

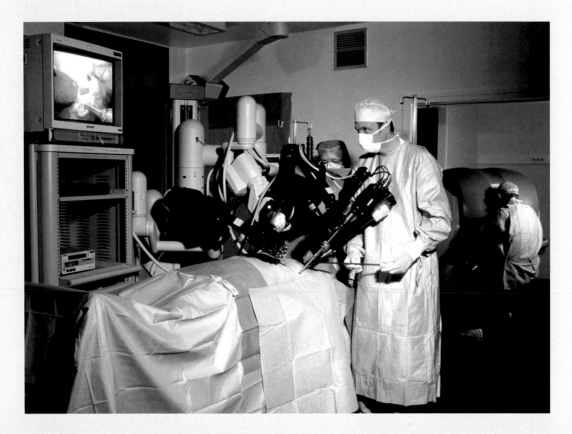

Many of these debates are based on what is ethically or morally right – for humans, for animals or for the environment. People often feel very strongly about such issues, whether they are governments, pressure groups or individuals. It is important for everyone to understand what these ethical questions are, and to consider the ways in which they might be solved.

Surgery has moved on from the times of crude although often effective knife-work of 200 years ago. Today surgeons work with anaesthetics, precision instruments and sophisticated electronics.

The role of the doctor

Living at the start of the twenty-first century, it is easy to think of medicine as a branch of science or technology, and to consider your doctor as a scientist, much as you would view a biologist or chemist. This is not entirely true. Doctors are certainly trained in science and they use it every day in their work, but they are also carers who respond to their patients' needs in many different ways.

Two hundred years ago the practice of medicine was unlikely to have been thought of as scientific at all – doctors were seen as practitioners of the healing arts. In those days, physicians might treat patients with herbs that they had collected and prepared themselves. Over the centuries, doctors have relied more and more on scientific research to develop new ways of treating patients. They have also increasingly expected the pharmaceutical and electronics industries to provide the drugs and tools that they need.

Developments in these areas have made life easier for many, but they have also raised ethical questions that were not considered in the past. These include how far we should go in treating certain diseases, who should receive such treatment if resources are limited, as well as issues about the ways in which medical research is carried out.

Global healthcare

It is important to remember that the same medical options are not available for everyone. An illness that can be treated with drugs or surgery in North America or Western Europe may still be fatal in less developed countries, where such options are often not available. Many healthcare workers and scientists believe that too much emphasis is placed on treating disease, and more time and money must be spent on preventative medicine. In the developed world this may take the form of encouraging people to eat less and exercise more, but in developing countries these points are not appropriate and instead the focus may be on vaccination programmes or improving hygiene.

This book looks at some of the changes taking place in healthcare today and the dilemmas these developments have raised. It is the responsibility of us all to decide how we can influence decisions relating to these issues.

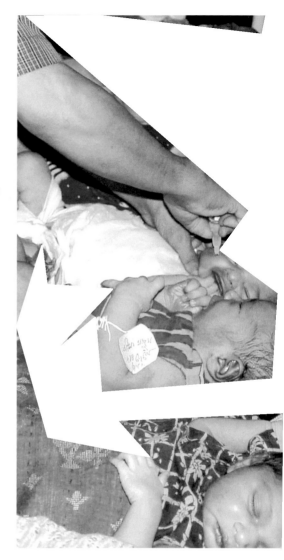

In developed countries diseases like polio are a thing of the past, but in less developed countries such as India, immunisation programmes are still working towards this goal.

 Ethical Care

We all need medical help at some time in our lives – it may be that we fall ill, suffer a sports injury, have a baby or simply need a check-up. When we come into contact with doctors, nurses and other health professionals we have to trust them.

Medical science is constantly changing and new developments are being made all the time; health professionals are expected to keep up to date with these developments. We expect the drugs they prescribe to be as safe as possible. We also expect that the instruments they use for diagnosis will be accurate and that their readings will be correctly interpreted.

Ethical codes

All this is a lot to ask of our doctors, yet they rarely let us down. We also demand something equally important from them – that they treat us ethically at all times. We assume they will be truthful and helpful, and we do not expect them to discuss our case with anyone inappropriately, or be careless with our records and personal details. If we were very ill we would not expect our doctors to stop treating us, or do anything that would deliberately harm us. Our society has developed a system of ethics in which the practice of medicine is entirely devoted to keeping people well and treating them if they fall ill.

All ethical codes and systems are based on morals – beliefs that something we do is right or wrong. Morals that have become part of an official code of behaviour are called ethics. Some people's morals are drawn from their religious beliefs, while others develop them from the influence of their parents or from their own interpretation of the world. For a moral belief to become part of an ethical code, there has to be wide agreement upon it in the society of the time.

Hippocrates is known as the 'father of medicine'. As well as formulating the ethical code known as the Hippocratic Oath (see opposite), his ideas on the causes of disease were revolutionary.

This illuminated manuscript shows an early version of the Hippocratic Oath. Medical students today take a modern form of the Oath when they have completed their training. In this, they vow to observe doctor-patient confidentiality and to treat all their patients the best they can.

The Hippocratic Oath

In ancient Greece, a doctor called Hippocrates (406–377 BC, see page 8) put together a set of principles for doctors called the Hippocratic Oath. When doctors completed their training they would take the Oath, by which they pledged themselves to the honest and careful treatment of their patients. Today most doctors still take some form of modern Hippocratic Oath, committing themselves to the same ethical code as those ancient Greek doctors.

THE OATH AND MODERN MEDICINE

Some people believe that medical practice has changed so much since the Oath was devised that it is no longer relevant, even in its modern form. Others argue that such a commitment to ethical standards is more important than ever in these days of new and powerful technologies. Should the Oath be abandoned altogether or is it still an important code of conduct for doctors?

❝ *I will remember that there is art to medicine as well as science, and that warmth, sympathy and understanding may outweigh the surgeon's knife or the chemist's drug. I will not be ashamed to say 'I know not', nor will I fail to call in my colleagues when the skills of another are needed for a patient's recovery. I will remember that I remain a member of society, with special obligations to all my fellow human beings, those sound of mind and body as well as the infirm.* ❞

Modern version of the Hippocratic Oath

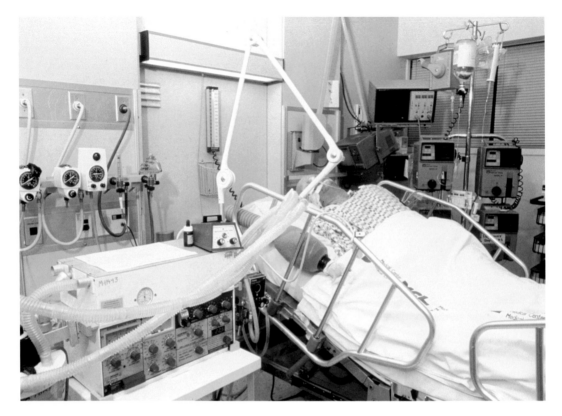

Life-support machines can keep people alive, sometimes indefinitely, even when all chance of recovery has gone. When should these machines be switched off? And who should make that choice – the family or the doctor?

" *There is often a tension between respecting the patient's religious beliefs and pursuing the patient's best interests.* **"**

Dr Farr Curlin
Maclean Center for Clinical Medical Ethics

The right to life

The kind of treatment individuals expect from their doctors may seem like a simple issue, but in fact a large number of people are involved in what might appear to be the smallest of medical decisions. Most countries have distinct laws that relate to what doctors can do. These laws derive from different places in different cultures, but many of them have their roots in religion. Several medical codes – and the ethical issues they give rise to – come from religious books such as the Torah, the Bible and the Qur'an.

One of the most controversial topics in medicine today is who decides when a life is over. Life-support machines and drugs can keep people alive when in the past they would have died. In situations where patients are suffering or have no hope of long-term recovery, doctors and families face the question of whether or not treatment should be withdrawn. Most religions prohibit the taking of life. Is switching off a life-support machine taking life, or is it helping the patient to a peaceful and pain-free death?

This map shows the percentage of total government expenditure that goes on healthcare across the world. In some areas very little state money goes on caring for the sick.

Expenditure (%)

● 2–4.9 ● 5–9.9 ● 10–14.9 ● 15–19.9 ○ 20 and higher ○ Data not available

Personal choices

It is not just a patient's religious views that have to be considered. Some doctors will have personal moral views that may affect the type of treatment they are prepared to offer. Roman Catholic doctors may not want to prescribe contraceptives because these are prohibited by their religion. Jewish and Islamic doctors may not want to use drugs based on pork products. These views may be completely different to those held by the patient. Patients' views may also prevent doctors from giving them the treatment that they need; a vegetarian patient may refuse to take drugs that have been made from animal products, for example. Should the treatment offered be based on the beliefs of the doctor or the patient?

The cost and availability of treatment

Treatment today may involve expensive drugs and other forms of care. In countries like the United Kingdom, where the state provides medical care, does the government have a right to withhold drugs in some cases? A new drug may take many years to develop and test (see pages 12–17), but drug companies also need to make a profit. The ethical issues surrounding whether or not drugs should be available to all are complex. Sometimes only those living in more developed countries can afford certain drugs, and many people in less developed countries have diseases that they cannot afford to treat. Is it ethical for them to be deprived of treatment just because of its cost?

YOU DECIDE

The ethical decisions that doctors have to make can be difficult and many may seem hard to match to a statement in the Hippocratic Oath.

? *A patient may not want treatment on religious grounds, even if it is the best course of action. How can doctors to deal with this without compromising the patient's moral beliefs?*

? *Several patients may be in need of a liver transplant, but only one liver is available. How should doctors decide who receives the liver transplant?*

? *How should doctors cope with situations where they are required to offer treatments with which they morally disagree?*

2 Drugs and Drug Testing

Drugs have been used for thousands of years to cure diseases and help control pain. For most of this time the drugs were not tested at all, and a trial-and-error system was used to judge their effectiveness and discover any side-effects. Today, however, there are strict laws governing how medical drugs should be tested and when they are made available to the public. Some of the most heated debates at the moment are those relating to the use and testing of drugs.

Herbal medicines like these are still used today for their healing properties. Modern drugs, however, require stringent testing before they can be given to patients.

Why do we need to test drugs?

Trial and error would not be suitable for today's drugs for a number of reasons. To begin with, these drugs are usually developed by commercial pharmaceutical companies, which would face serious legal problems if their products were found to be dangerous or ineffective. To avoid this, they spend a lot of time and money making sure their products are safe.

In the past, many substances used for treating illnesses were prepared directly from plants – some of these herbal remedies, such as St John's Wort, raspberry-leaf 'tea' and senna, are still used today and are not subject to scientific testing. However, most modern drugs are extremely powerful compared with herbal remedies, so it is vital to get the dosage right and identify unwanted side-effects.

As modern drugs began to be developed, testing usually took place on the scientists who had worked on the drug as well as a few volunteers, but other ways of drug testing were later used. Today, any new drug must go through a series of tests that is likely to involve several stages, including testing on animals and humans – healthy volunteers and those who take part in clinical trials to have their diseases treated with a new medication. The process from early development of a drug to its widespread and accepted use can take many years.

Millions of pounds are spent on drugs research by large companies every year.

The advantages of animals in drug-testing

Using animals for drug testing is an issue that provokes strong reactions in people. Traditionally, the animals most often used in drug research were rats and guinea pigs, but cats, dogs and monkeys have also been used. There are several advantages to using animals in drugs trials:

■ *It is possible to use large numbers of animals because they are more readily available than human volunteers.*
■ *Animals can be used at an earlier stage in drug development, when the possible dangers are not yet understood.*
■ *Animals can be killed after the tests to see what effect the drugs have had on their internal organs.*
■ *The effect of drugs on the lifespan of the animals and the possible effects on future generations can be discovered in quite a short amount of time.*

Groups such as the Foundation for Biomedical Research in America and the Research Defence Society in the United Kingdom support the use of animals in drug testing. They say that without it, medicines such as insulin (for diabetes) and antibiotics (for infectious diseases) would not be available to the millions of people that rely on them.

" *It's vitally important that the research community sends the message that animal research is crucial for medical progress, that it is conducted humanely, and that we work within strict regulations.* **"**

Nancy Rothwell
Chairman of the Research Defence Society (UK)

13

Objections to animal testing

Many people disagree strongly with the use of animals in drug trials. The main objections to animal testing are:

- *Animals are not humans, and drugs are unlikely to act in the same way or produce the same side-effects as they would if tested on humans.*
- *Drug testing on animals involves unnecessary suffering, which is not justified.*
- *Human volunteers are willing participants in drug trials, but animals are unable to give their consent.*
- *The regulations controlling animal testing in parts of the world are not strict enough.*
- *Alternatives to animal testing exist and should be further developed.*

There are many organisations all over the world that use these arguments in their campaigns against animal testing of any kind. There is, however, an important distinction to be made between using animals to test drugs that may help to cure diseases in humans, and using animals to test cosmetics and toiletries that are not essential to human life.

> **Because of the irreconcilable biological differences between animals and human beings, the results of animal tests cannot be applied to human beings with any degree of confidence.**
>
> *Dr Andre Menache*
> *World Congress on Law and Medicine*

Animals such as rats are kept in cages in laboratories and monitored for any effects that the drugs may have on them.

People protest about animal testing because they consider such treatment cruel and unnecessary.

Animal-rights activists

Animal-rights activists are people that strongly object to animal testing and organise campaigns to make sure their views are heard by the bodies that control policies on animal research. On occasion some individuals within the animal-rights movement have broken the law in order to further their aims. Some research establishments have stopped using animals in their testing because of pressure from animal-rights activists. Activists have been pleased at the results of these protests, but supporters of animal research argue that such campaigns will force animal testing to be conducted in countries where regulations are not so strict, and this might result in greater animal suffering. Pressure from animal-rights groups has resulted in laws being changed to offer animals greater protection. For example, in 2002 the German government amended the country's constitution to include animal welfare.

> **ANIMAL PROTECTION**
> *In 2002, the German constitution (the code of laws of a country's government) was amended to read: 'The state takes responsibility for protecting the natural foundations of life and animals in the interests of future generations.' The addition of the words 'and animals' was seen as a big step forward by animal-rights activists.*

YOU DECIDE

The issue of supporting or objecting to animal testing is a very personal one and provokes strong reactions.

? *If a new drug was discovered that might be used to treat a life-threatening disease like cancer or HIV/AIDS, would you be happy for it to be used on humans without full trials on animals first?*

? *Should all animal testing be banned or just the testing that uses them for non-medical research such as cosmetics?*

? *Is it acceptable for activists to break the law because they are campaigning for a cause they believe in?*

Human drug trials

Once a drug has been tested on animals and any dangers eliminated, human trials can begin. Many new drugs are tested using 'double blind testing', in which the drug is given to some volunteers while a 'dummy' drug (called a placebo) is given to others. In a blind trial the volunteers do not know which they have been given; in a double blind trial, neither the volunteers nor the researchers know who has been given the active drug, although the drugs have been coded so researchers can find out later.

Regulatory bodies called ethics committees (Europe) or institutional review boards (USA) make sure that clinical trials are strictly regulated so that the risks to human subjects are minimal.

YOU DECIDE

In some countries, prisoners are given the chance to reduce their sentences by participating in unpaid drug trials.

? *Is it right that someone who has been found guilty of a crime can reduce their sentence in this way?*

? *How might this affect the victims of the crime?*

? *If prisoners are willing to take the risks of participating in drug trials, should they be paid like other volunteers?*

This young girl suffers from asthma. She is taking part in a voluntary clinical trial to find new ways of treating the illness.

Voluntary drug tests

There are many difficulties and controversies involved with human testing. To begin with, volunteers must be fit and healthy, and not taking any medication that might interfere with the new drug. They are often paid for the time that a trial takes. Critics of the system argue that volunteers are never really aware of the risks involved and that they may have their health permanently damaged. Supporters argue that no one is forcing them to participate.

When things go wrong

Although there are many safeguards in place to ensure drug trials present no danger to the subjects, there have been several high-profile cases of clinical trials going wrong, and this has made it a very controversial issue.

A drug called thalidomide was developed in the mid-twentieth century to help control morning sickness in pregnant women. Although the drug had undergone extensive trials on animals and volunteers, it later proved to have devastating side-effects. Many of the babies were born with no arms or legs and with hands and feet joined directly to their bodies, as well as other deformities.

The result of this case was that the American regulatory body the FDA (Food and Drug Administration) was given more control over human drug trials. Methods of conducting such tests have certainly improved since then, but there are still cases of trials going wrong.

Drug trials in the United Kingdom made world headlines in 2006 when six volunteers who had been given a drug quickly developed serious side-effects involving the failure of most body systems. Fortunately the trials were being carried out in a laboratory attached to a hospital, so emergency treatment was close at hand and none of the volunteers died. An official enquiry found that although there were some failures in clinical practice during the trial, no rules had been broken and the events were an accident that could not have been foreseen.

Incidents like this have raised many questions about how thoroughly – and indeed, how – drugs are tested before they are released to the public. As a result of these events it is likely that all the procedures of drug testing will be looked at again.

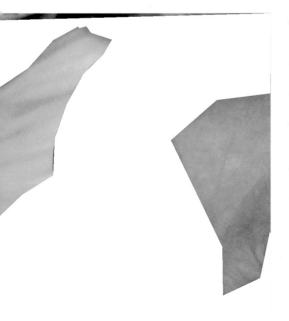

Many children whose mothers had taken the drug thalidomide were born with deformities in their limbs, as shown here in the hand and forearm. The thalidomide scandal brought the dangers of human trials to the attention of the world.

TGN1412

The substance involved in the UK drug trials that went terribly wrong was TGN1412, a new type of immune stimulant that had never been used in humans. Tests of TGN1412 in monkeys revealed no major side-effects. All six human subjects nearly died; within minutes of receiving the drug the volunteers were racked by chills, pain and nausea, and swelling of the head and limbs. Months after the trial the volunteers were still very ill.

This is the molecule of the substance TGN1412. The participants of the trial involving this drug are all likely to suffer lifelong health problems.

❝ The adverse incidents did not involve errors in the manufacture of TGN1412 or in its formulation, dilution or administration to trial participants. ❞

Report by the Medicines and Healthcare Products Regulatory Agency (MHRA)

Organ Transplants

The first successful transplant of part of a human body was probably performed in Vienna in 1905. Eduard Zirm transplanted corneas from eyes removed from one patient on to the damaged eyes of another patient. Since then, transplant surgery has been refined and developed, and has saved thousands of lives. However, there are also many ethical questions surrounding organ transplants, including where donor organs come from, and who they should go to.

This diagram shows the organs and tissues that can now be used in transplants. Some organs, such as a kidney, can be taken from a live donor, but others must come from people who have just died.

BODY PARTS

All organisms are made of cells, and those cells join together to form tissue. In turn, tissue makes up organs and those organs make up systems. For example, cardiac cells make up cardiac muscle and cardiac muscle makes up most of the heart. The heart is part of the circulatory system.

1. Eyes/corneas
2. Heart and heart valves
3. Lungs
4. Liver
5. Kidneys
6. Pancreas
7. Intestines
8. Femoral and saphenous veins
9. Skin
10. Bone
11. Tendons

The development of transplant surgery

More sophisticated transplants first took place later in the twentieth century, including the kidney in 1954 and the liver in 1967. The first heart transplant also took place in 1967, performed by Dr Christiaan Barnard in South Africa. Since then, other organs and body parts have been transplanted, including hands and, in 2005, the first full face transplant for a woman who had been badly bitten in the face by a dog. Today, transplants are commonplace in most developed countries.

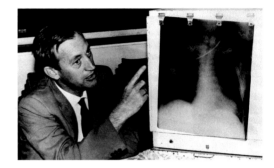

South African surgeon Dr Christiaan Barnard explains the procedure he used to perform the first heart transplant in 1967.

❝ *I expect to resume a normal life… I pay homage to the donor's family. My operation could help others to live again.* **❞**

Isabelle Dinoire
Recipient of the first full face transplant

Donors and recipients

It is easy to consider the surgical process in terms of remarkable surgeons and expert techniques. Heart and lung transplants have undeniably given many years of active life to thousands of people. However, the development of this type of surgery has followed many years of animal experiments and failed surgeries on humans. Even today, undergoing transplant surgery is risky. For a transplant to succeed, usually a donor and a recipient must be matched in terms of tissue type. An organ that is transplanted from one person to another will be rejected if the recipient's immune system attacks it. The choices that must be made by both recipients and donors – or their families – raise several ethical questions.

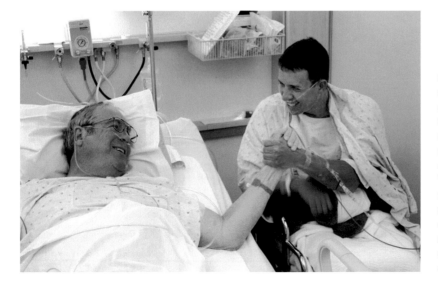

Finding live donors who match recipients can be difficult. These two men were matched for a kidney transplant through a commercial website. This method of matching caused a debate about the ethics of organ matching through commercial organisations.

How organs are obtained

There are two ways of obtaining organs for transplants. In the case of kidneys, healthy donors can donate one of their kidneys to someone of very close tissue type – usually a family member. However, in most cases of transplant surgery the organ cannot be donated in this way. People only have one heart, one pancreas and one liver. The second way of obtaining organs is by taking a healthy organ from a donor who has recently died. If he or she has died from illness or disease the organ is unlikely to be in a good enough condition, so the victims of accidents are often used for donations.

This raises a big ethical problem. If the donor is dead, how can he or she give consent for an organ to be taken? Time is short – in most cases, the organ must be removed quickly and kept in cold conditions until the recipient is prepared. This leaves only a small window of opportunity for surgeons to use organs for transplant.

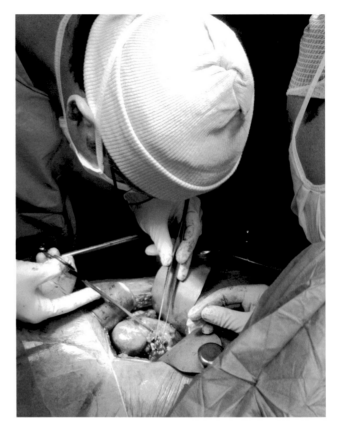

Surgeons performing a kidney transplant. Such transplants can be done using live donors because humans have two kidneys but are able to function with just one.

Voluntary organ donation

One answer to this problem is the use of a donor card. People can carry a card with them, so that in the event of an accident, their organs can be quickly removed. It makes clear their wishes to be a donor in the event of their death. Another alternative is to have a national register of organ donors held on a central computer, so the identity of the accident victim can be found quickly and organs removed. In some parts of the world, driving licences show whether the owner is willing to donate organs in case of an accident.

Consent for organ donation

In many countries at the moment, the families of people who are killed in accidents and who do not carry donor cards are asked for permission to remove organs. This raises

> 66 *Although the 'gift of life' discourse may remain useful in heightening public awareness about the benefits of donation, this is not an adequate framework for understanding what is important for the family at the bedside faced with a donation decision.* 99

Report by the UK Transplant Organisation

Doctors have to work quickly after an accident if the victim's organs are to be used for transplant. They are carefully removed while the recipient is prepared for surgery so that the transfer can be made as swiftly as possible.

questions about who really has the right to grant this kind of permission. Some people argue that only donors themselves can give this consent, and that even the family does not have the right to grant it. Critics also point out that this is a very difficult time for the family and there are cases where loved-ones have felt pressured to make a decision quickly. Health workers have to use a great deal of tact and understanding to get their permission. Supporters of this kind of donation argue that knowing someone has helped another person to live after their death can be a great comfort to bereaved families. They are often glad they have agreed to the organ donation.

Even with such systems in place there is an organ shortage. A new system has been suggested in which people would carry a document stating that they *don't* give consent. Without this, it would be assumed that they are willing to donate organs. Is it right to make such an assumption, or should either decision be clearly stated?

YOU DECIDE

Deciding whether or not to donate your organs after death is a big decision and a very personal choice.

? *Do you think that people should carry organ-transplant cards if they want to donate organs, or should a new card be introduced for people who do not want to donate organs?*

? *Why do you think that some families do not allow the organs of a relative to be used for transplant?*

? *What happens if an accident victim is found to be carrying an organ-donor card, but relatives refuse to allow medical professionals to act on this?*

The shortage of organs

Due to the shortage of organs, there are often waiting lists of patients needing a specific type of organ. When one organ of a certain tissue type becomes available, how do healthcare professionals choose who the recipient will be? They literally have to decide who has the chance to live and who may die.

Usually, some kind of 'points' system is used by health workers, and the patient with the most points will end up with the best chance of receiving the organ. Factors taken into consideration include:

- *Age of recipient.*
- *General state of health.*
- *Specific health problems, HIV/AIDS, heart conditions etc.*
- *Dependent relatives.*
- *History of drug and alcohol abuse.*
- *Chances of successful transplant.*
- *Life expectancy after the transplant.*

A particular area of difficulty is the number of alcoholics that need a liver transplant. The liver is easily damaged by alcoholism and a transplant offers a way of extending life to somebody with a damaged liver. Should doctors ensure that patients have given up alcohol before going ahead with the transplant? If a person has damaged their liver by choosing to drink too much, should he or she receive a donated organ when there is a shortage of livers?

This human liver has been damaged by hepatitis and cirrhosis, both caused by alcohol abuse. Extensive damage like this means that a new liver must be found.

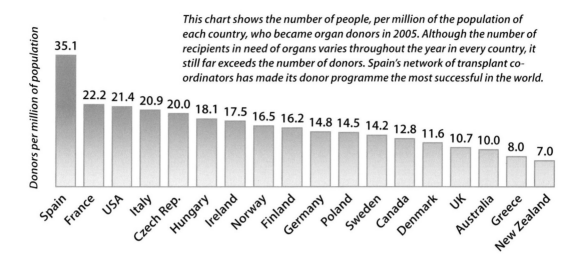

This chart shows the number of people, per million of the population of each country, who became organ donors in 2005. Although the number of recipients in need of organs varies throughout the year in every country, it still far exceeds the number of donors. Spain's network of transplant co-ordinators has made its donor programme the most successful in the world.

Xenotransplantation

Xenotransplantation is the name given to the process of transferring organs from one species to another. Work has been undertaken that has enabled animals such as pigs to be bred that have human-compatible organs for transplant. These animals are the result of cloning research (see pages 30–35). While this has the potential for solving the problem of a shortage of donors, it does raise a number of ethical issues. Is it right to put animal organs into humans? Suppose that new diseases develop in animals and these can be passed on to humans because of the tissue type? Obviously this is a difficult area for those who must create ethical codes. Animal-rights activists are unhappy with the use of animals in this way.

" *It is well established that most new emerging human infectious diseases generally have their origins in other species. A direct method of establishing new infectious human disease would be to implant infected tissues from a non-human species into humans.* **"**

Dr John Allen, on the potential risks of xenotransplantation
Southwest Foundation for Biomedical Research, USA

YOU DECIDE

There are systems in place to ensure a distribution of organs based on medical criteria, but some people have found ways to 'jump the queue'.

? *Should transplant surgery be performed on a 'first come first served' basis?*

? *Should the families of donors have a say in who donated organs go to?*

? *Is it fair that in many cases older donor recipients lose out to younger ones in the selection process?*

4 Genetic Engineering

Genetic engineering has developed dramatically in the past few years. Scientists now understand a great deal about how genes work and can use this knowledge to manipulate them for the benefit of human health. However, genetic engineering has given rise to some of the greatest dilemmas in recent medical research, in particular how genetic technology can be applied ethically and who really 'owns' an individual's genetic information.

What are genes?

The human body is made up of trillions of cells. Each cell contains 46 chromosomes. Each chromosome is composed of genes, and those genes are made up of sections of DNA. DNA is a molecule that contains the genetic code for life. All the variations that can be seen from one person to another are expressions of differences in the make-up of the genes in particular chromosomes. Most people have the right combination of genes to live a long and healthy life, but some individuals have 'faulty genes', which lack the information needed to make important proteins. Lacking such proteins will result in a genetic disorder.

The Human Genome Project investigates the sequence of the human DNA code. Here, a technician loads a DNA sample into a sequencer.

If we knew the exact function of each chromosome in the human body it would be possible to screen people for genetic disorders. It might also be possible to find out whether certain human characteristics, such as intelligence, are a result of a certain mix of genes. There are many supporters of research into genetics.

The Human Genome Project

The Human Genome Project was started in 1990. Its aims were:

- *To identify all the approximately 20,000–25,000 genes that make up human chromosomes.*
- *To determine the sequences of the code that makes up the DNA in humans.*
- *To store this information in databases.*
- *To improve tools for data analysis.*
- *To transfer related technologies to the private sector, and address the ethical, legal and social issues that may arise from the project.*

While the original aim was to complete the main body of work by 2003, it is now expected to continue for many years to come. In particular, the last of the aims contains the basis of many important ethical debates.

Those involved in the project hope that the information gained will help the millions of people who suffer from genetic diseases such as cystic fibrosis or sickle-cell anaemia. However, others fear that the information gained from the project will be misused and that attempts will be made to change the genetic make-up of individuals in order to develop 'desirable' characteristics. Most of those opposed to genetic engineering see no point to the Human Genome Project other than the manipulation of genes, and therefore think it is wrong. Others feel that the information could be important in helping prospective parents find out whether their children will suffer from a genetic disorder.

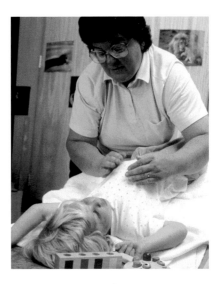

Cystic fibrosis is a genetic disorder that affects the lungs. Sufferers usually need to have regular therapy to loosen the mucus that builds up in their lungs so they can breathe properly.

DRUGS FROM GENES

Genes from the chromosomes of humans (and other organisms) can be extracted using enzymes, and then transferred to a bacterial cell. The bacterium in the cell is then genetically engineered on a large scale to produce significant amounts of a protein. This method is used to manufacture important drugs and hormones for medicinal use, including human insulin. The Human Genome Project could enable the manufacture of the missing proteins that cause many genetic disorders.

YOU DECIDE

Some people think that genetic engineering is taking modern medicine a step too far.

? *Is it right for doctors and scientists to interfere with the genetic make-up of individuals?*

? *If we have the ability to 'cure' diseases like cystic fibrosis, shouldn't we be doing all that we can to help?*

? *Is 'going against nature' a valid argument against genetic engineering?*

Amniocentesis is a form of genetic screening during pregnancy, in which some of the fluid surrounding the unborn child is extracted. The cells are then tested for genetic or chromosomal disorders. Amniocentesis carries a risk of causing miscarriage.

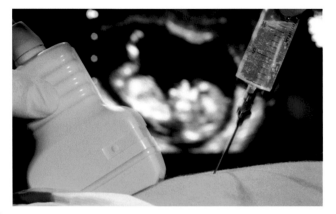

66 *Clinics must be satisfied about the welfare of the future child. It's not social engineering, it's being responsible.* **99**

Suzi Leather
Chair of the UK Human Fertilisation and Embryology Authority

YOU DECIDE

Some people argue that genetic screening is a matter for health carers and parents, but others say it is a question for governments.

? *Who should pay for the screening programme – the individuals who want it or governments?*

? *Do the benefits associated with genetic screening outweigh the potential risks?*

? *What types of genetic disorders should be included in screening programmes?*

What is genetic screening?

Genetic screening is when adults are tested for genetic disorders either before or during pregnancy. Such disorders range from fairly common variations such as colour-blindness, to serious diseases like cystic fibrosis or haemophilia. Many parents who have genetic disorders in their families are screened before they decide to have children, or they have tests soon after the woman becomes pregnant to find out if the developing foetus has any abnormalities.

The problems associated with genetic screening

In many cases genetic screening can assure people that their children are not at great risk of genetic disorders. The ethical problems arise when screening shows that a child might be susceptible to a disorder. This knowledge can present parents with difficult decisions about whether to have children at all, or whether to proceed with a pregnancy.

Those who support screening argue that it makes sense to discover if any children would have defects that might make their lives difficult. Objectors to screening believe that there is an ethical line that might be crossed. As our understanding of genetics increases, it might one day be possible for parents to decide what kind of baby they would like and to reject any foetuses that do not match this ideal. This could include choosing the sex or hair and eye colour of the child. Newspapers have labelled these 'designer babies'. Where do we draw the line between manipulating genes to create a healthy baby, and doing so to encourage characteristics that are not related to health and well-being?

Genetic testing

Genetic screening is not the same as genetic testing. In genetic testing, babies have some blood taken soon after birth and this is then tested for a number of genetic disorders. If the parents know about any genetic abnormalities they can make plans early in the child's life. In countries where infants are tested for cystic fibrosis, the child has a much better chance of receiving appropriate treatment. In countries where this test is not carried out, children might reach eight or nine years of age before the disease is diagnosed and any suitable treatment is made available. The ethical issues associated with genetic testing are largely related to who should have access to the results of such tests (see pages 28–29) and how it should be regulated on both national and international levels. The World Health Organization, in association with other groups such as the European Commission, has been trying to develop an international set of regulations to govern how tests should be carried out in both developed and developing countries.

In South Korea, scientists have found a way of cloning human embryos (pictured). They hope that these embryos will help with medical research and say the embryos will never develop beyond an early stage, but now we know how to do this, where will human cloning end?

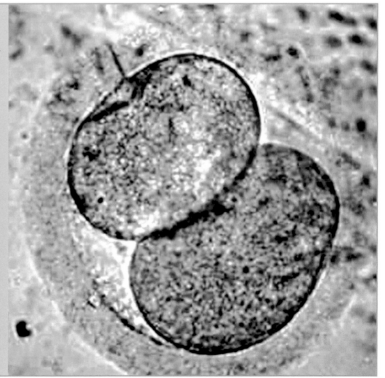

CLONING

Cloning is a particular area of genetic engineering that has been the subject of much debate. The process of cloning involves taking genetic material from one organism and using it to create a genetically identical copy of it. In 1996, scientists successfully cloned a mammal for the first time. Dolly the sheep's birth was seen as a remarkable step forward for science by some people – and a terrifyingly dangerous move by others. Cloning humans is, in theory, no more difficult than cloning sheep.

The future of genetic engineering

From the first work carried out on the structure of the nucleus of the cell, through to cracking the genetic code all the way, the Human Genome Project has been a journey of a little over 100 years. The next century will be a time of intense discovery of our genetic make-up. Genetic screening and DNA manipulation may occur and this could affect the future evolution of our species.

Throughout the history of science, new discoveries have always had ethical issues associated with them; genetics raises more of these issues than most other themes because it relates to who we are and who our children will be. The chances are we may be able to choose a whole range of characteristics about our children in the future, but are these steps we wish to take? Even if we are able to choose the sex of our baby, what would be the consequences on our society?

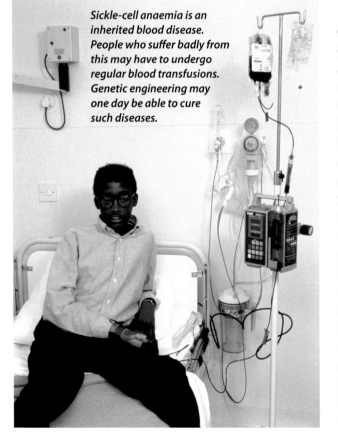

Sickle-cell anaemia is an inherited blood disease. People who suffer badly from this may have to undergo regular blood transfusions. Genetic engineering may one day be able to cure such diseases.

Who owns the information?

One other consequence of improved genetic understanding is that large amounts of genetic information about individuals is being collected and stored. The question of who should hold this information and who should have access to it is a major ethical dilemma. Over the past decade or so genetic fingerprinting has been used to solve crimes by identifying body material such as blood or saliva. If DNA records are held by health professionals, should they be as confidential as medical records, or should they be made available to other authorities for the good of society? If parents discover they have a genetic disorder, are they morally obliged to tell their children in case it has been passed to them, or do they have the right to keep the information to themselves?

Genetic discrimination

One of the biggest concerns relates to possible discrimination against people if their genetic information is known. For example, a health-insurance company might not give you insurance if it knew you were at risk of a genetic disorder. Is this fair? Companies have to protect themselves, but should individuals suffer as a result? There are other social implications, too. For example, employers might not offer a job to a person they knew was likely to suffer health problems in the future.

The availability of genetic information is perhaps not as strictly controlled as it should be and many countries have set up committees or other organisations – such as the US Secretary's Advisory Committee on Genetics, Health, and Society – to look into cases of genetic discrimination.

Everyone has a different DNA sequence, which looks a bit like a barcode when it is visualised. This DNA 'fingerprint' has many social uses – from identifying criminals to paternity testing.

YOU DECIDE

Genetic manipulation throws up many difficult decisions for parents and for society as a whole.

? *If parents know that they carry a serious genetic disorder that only affects boys, should they be allowed to use genetic testing to ensure they have only female children?*

? *Is it possible to prevent the new power of genetic manipulation from being abused by those who have political ideas about how the human race should be changed?*

? *Where should the line be drawn between what is allowable and what should be controlled?*

❝ *This new knowledge should be seen as a blessing and not a curse, because it opens up the way to the development of new medicines that can be used by all people, everywhere.* **❞**

Dr Mike Dexter
Director of the Wellcome Trust

5 Stem-Cell Research

Stem cells are an important component of medical research today and many serious medical conditions, like cancer and birth defects, may be treated by stem-cell therapy. However, the source of these stem cells and the way they are used during research has resulted in powerful ethical debates between researchers and human-rights groups. The potential benefits of stem-cell research are enormous, but does this justify the way they are harvested?

What are stem cells?

Cells are the basic building blocks of life. Very simple organisms may be made up of only one kind of cell, whereas larger, more complex organisms like humans are made up of trillions of cells. Most of the cells in a multicellular organism have a specialised function, such as liver cells, brain cells and blood cells. Some cells have the ability to develop into any of these specialised cells and these are called stem cells. They act as a repair system for the body and can, in theory, divide without limit to replace other cells as long as the person or animal is still alive. When a stem cell divides, each new cell has the potential to either remain a stem cell or become a cell with a more specialised function.

Stem cells can be used in many different areas of health and medical research, and studying them can help scientists to understand how stem cells transform into the tissues and organs that make us what we are.

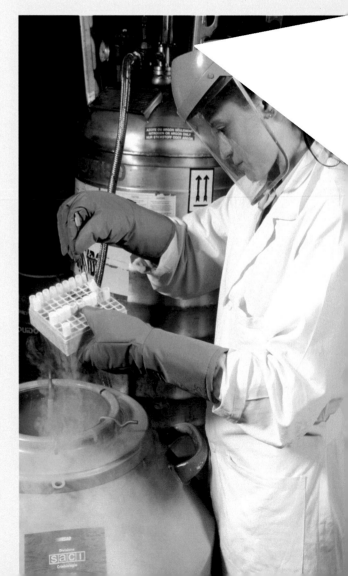

Stem cells have to be stored very carefully after they have been harvested. They are kept in liquid nitrogen at −182°C to preserve them.

Embryonic stem cells

The ethical debate about stem-cell research revolves around where these cells come from.

Many of them are taken from a developing embryo – embryonic stem cells. Gathering the cells involves the splitting apart of cells from a developing embryo before they become specialised. Embryonic stem cells are taken from embryos that develop from eggs which have been fertilised outside the mother's body in a laboratory (*in vitro fertilisation*) and then donated for research purposes with the consent of the donors. The embryos from which human embryonic stem cells are derived are usually five days old and are a hollow microscopic ball of cells called a blastocyst. Most of the women who donate eggs are receiving fertility treatment and in some countries these are the only permitted source of embryonic stem cells.

EMBRYONIC CLONES

Research has shown that stem cells can be used to produce clones; embryonic stem cells are split up into two, producing two embryos. The identical embryos that are produced are implanted into different host mothers, to produce identical offspring.

A blastocyst is a hollow ball of cells formed by cell division shortly after an egg has been fertilised. It is the very first stage of embryonic development.

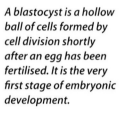 *Cloning may be good and it may be bad. Probably it's a bit of both. The question must not be greeted with reflex hysteria but decided quietly, soberly and on its own merits. We need less emotion and more thought.* 💬

Richard Dawkins
Scientist

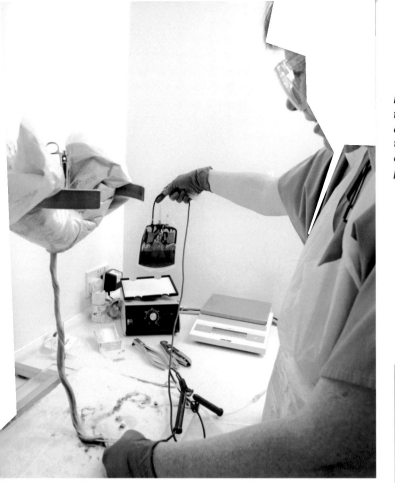

Here, stem cells are being collected from an umbilical cord immediately after birth. This is less controversial than sourcing stem cells from embryos. Parents can 'donate' the placenta and cord for this purpose.

The debate about embryonic research

People who oppose embryonic stem-cell research believe that embryos are living things and should be treated with the same respect for life as humans. They argue that although the research has promised many medical benefits, the advances have, as yet, not been sufficient to justify the research methods. Other methods of research have been found (see below) so these should be used instead. Supporters of embryonic research claim that the embryos would be destroyed anyway, and that using them to harvest stem cells could have huge medical benefits for millions of people. Although other methods have been developed, embryonic stem-cell research is still the most efficient.

Somatic stem cells

Adult stem cells (somatic stem cells) come from undifferentiated cells (cells that have not yet become specialised) from an animal. Scientists have found adult stem cells in many kinds of tissue. Adult blood-forming

YOU DECIDE

There are many different factors that affect people's opinions on stem-cell research.

? *Is it right that people famous for being movie stars or the wife of a president should have a public platform for their views on important ethical issues?*

? *Is it right that they can get their views across to the public when you might be unable to?*

? *If someone in your family was suffering from Parkinson's disease or some other disorder that might be helped by stem-cell research, how do you think this would influence your opinion in the debate?*

stem cells found in bone marrow have been used in transplants for many years. If the specialisation of adult stem cells can be controlled in the laboratory, these cells may become the basis of therapies for many serious common diseases. Adult stem cells are not as useful as embryonic stem cells because they seem to be less adaptable. One important use for adult stem cells is producing tissue from the patient that the cells have been taken from, for later transplant.

Famous supporters and opponents

Stem-cell research has been the cause of some very public debates. It touches on several areas about which individuals have strong opinions, such as the sanctity of human life, the limits of scientific involvement, and the lengths to which we should go to heal disease.

Some celebrities have involved themselves very firmly in this debate, in particular Michael J. Fox, who has had to give up acting due to Parkinson's disease. He sees stem-cell research as vital in producing cures that will help thousands of people live better lives. However, many people, including US President George W. Bush and his wife Laura, have very serious misgivings about it. Debates about using stem cells not from embryos but from aborted foetuses has caused even more controversy, as it has become part of the whole abortion debate.

This debate was highlighted at the end of 2006. Baby Amilia Taylor was born at just under 22 weeks – and survived. In many countries, women can choose to have an abortion up to 24 weeks. Amilia's birth reignited the debate about the point at which unborn babies should be accorded the same rights to life as anyone else.

> ❝ *If the potential of stem-cell research is realized, it would mean an end to the suffering of millions of people – a rescue, a cure… Stem cells could lead to breakthroughs in developing treatments and cures for almost any terminal or catastrophic disease you can think of… If stem-cell research succeeds, there isn't a person in the country who won't benefit, or know somebody who will.* ❞
>
> **Michael J. Fox**
> *Actor and campaigner*

Actor Michael J. Fox suffers from Parkinson's disease and has become a great supporter of stem-cell research.

33

Formulating an ethical code for stem-cell research

Because the issue has caused such controversy, governments all over the world have had to formulate policies on stem-cell research. The main areas of debate and discussion when developing these include the following:

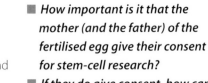

Controversy about stem-cell research is based around the question of when human life actually begins. If cells can be taken five weeks after fertilisation, why not six weeks or three months after fertilisation? Alternatively, is harvesting cells at any point after fertilisation taking a human life?

- *How important is it that the mother (and the father) of the fertilised egg give their consent for stem-cell research?*
- *If they do give consent, how can you be sure that they understand what they have agreed to?*
- *Should egg donors be paid?*
- *After fertilisation, to whom does the egg belong?*
- *As many fertilised eggs are often thrown away following* in vitro *fertilisation, why not use these eggs to provide stem cells? As these fertilised eggs have never been implanted in a woman's body can they be considered human life? Is it worth the risk that eggs will be fertilised unnecessarily in order to produce stem cells?*
- *Is it worth waiting for improvements in the use of adult stem cells, hoping that the need for embryonic stem cells will eventually become unnecessary?*
- *Should the products of stem-cell research be used for producing tissue and organs for transplants?*
- *Should the cloning of humans be allowed?*
- *What are the commercial implications of stem-cell research? Should it be funded by governments or by commercial companies? Is it right to allow public funds invested in universities and research establishments to be used in this way?*

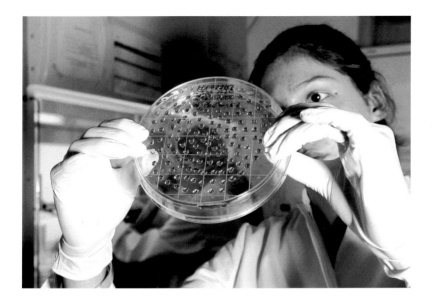

If research like this, on stem-cell cultures, can help develop treatments for debilitating diseases like Parkinson's, should there be more support for it, whatever the source of the cells?

International policies on stem-cell research

In putting forward laws and ethical codes, many questions have to be taken into account and, to some extent, this may be a reflection of the moral and religious heritage of individual countries. Countries that have passed laws which are generally considered to be liberal about stem-cell research include the United Kingdom, China, Israel and Iran. Embryonic stem-cell research is banned in many countries, including Germany, Ireland, Italy and Poland. In the United States, there is division between states – some have made it illegal, while others support this kind of research.

> **❝** *As I thought through this issue, I kept returning to two fundamental questions: First, are these frozen embryos human life, and therefore something precious to be protected? And second, if they're going to be destroyed anyway, shouldn't they be used for a greater good, for research that has the potential to save and improve other lives?* **❞**

George W. Bush

YOU DECIDE

Governments ruling on stem-cell research must recognise that if they reject it, then other countries may gain scientific and commercial advantage by going ahead.

? *Is this a good enough reason to endorse embryonic stem-cell research?*

? *Should a worldwide set of ethical considerations be drawn up to which all countries must adhere, rather than each country deciding its own course of action?*

Modern Medicine and You

It may seem that doctors and other health professionals are faced with difficult moral and ethical dilemmas when treating their patients. Of course that is true, but it is also true that even you will face some difficult decisions on a daily basis. With increased knowledge of those life choices that cause ill-health, we are the ones that need to decide what we do with our bodies.

The right to make decisions for other people

In the United States in 2006, the parents of a young girl went to court to get permission to give their daughter, Ashley, drugs that would prevent her growing into an adult. Ashley had a disease called static encephalopathy, which meant that her brain would never develop beyond that of a three-month-old baby. She would never be able to walk, talk or feed herself. Her parents argued that by limiting her growth they could offer her better care and save her from the discomforts of adult growth. They won the case, and it sparked a global debate about taking such action.

Many people agreed that in doing this her parents had helped improve her quality of life. Others said that they had

> **Ashley was dealt a challenging life and the least we could do as her loving parents and care-givers is to be diligent about maximising her quality of life.**
>
> *Ashley's father*

Should it be the responsibility of parents, healthcare workers or law courts to decide what is best for severely disabled children?

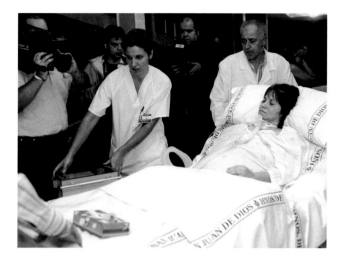

Inmaculada Echevarría Ramirez suffers from progressive muscular dystrophy, which means she is bedridden with no hope of recovery. She has asked for euthanasia, believing it is her right to choose how she should live – and die.

been looking after their own interests, that preventing Ashley from growing normally was cruel. The case forced many people to think about the rights we have to make decisions for others, and how far medical intervention should be taken.

Euthanasia

Improved medical techniques have introduced a difficult ethical issue for many doctors and for the relatives of patients who have serious diseases. Doctors can keep people alive with drugs and life support – but how far should this go? If a patient has passed the stage where they are ever going to recover, is there a point when the life-support systems should be switched off, and who decides when that point has been reached? Several cases have ended up in court when the medical profession and the family cannot agree on the best course of action.

Some patients who have serious and often painful medical conditions decide that they want to take their own lives. For many such people, this is not possible without help, so who, if anyone, should aid them in dying? In some countries, including Switzerland, the law allows individuals to die with medical help, but in most places this is illegal and any doctor or family member who assists in the process is likely to be charged with murder. Most doctors would want the law to be very clear about this difficult area. Others might have religious or other beliefs that would prevent them from taking part in any unnecessary death.

YOU DECIDE

At the moment euthanasia is illegal in most countries, but there is increasing pressure to allow assisted suicide in some circumstances.

? *Should people be forced to stay alive when their quality of life is vastly reduced and they have expressed a desire to die while they are still able to make that decision?*

? *What are the arguments for and against euthanasia?*

? *Should the cost of healthcare for terminally ill patients or those with degenerative diseases be a factor in whether or not to legalise euthanasia and assisted suicide?*

Type II diabetes – sometimes called adult-onset diabetes – can be caused by eating too much sugar (although this is not the only cause). Patients will have to use expensive drugs for the rest of their lives. Should people take more responsibility for their lifestyles to prevent such diseases?

The right to decide for ourselves

It is not only other people's lives that we might one day have to make decisions about. Every day we make decisions about our own health. Below are a number of issues that you can make choices about:

- *Taking too little exercise may lead to obesity and heart disease.*
- *Eating too much sugar may cause obesity and Type II diabetes.*
- *Smoking cigarettes may cause cancer and lung disease.*
- *Eating a low-fibre diet may cause bowel cancer.*
- *Taking illegal drugs may cause addiction and problems with mental health.*
- *Unprotected sex may lead to HIV/AIDS and other sexually transmitted diseases.*
- *Drinking too much alcohol may lead to liver disease and alcoholism.*

YOU DECIDE

The arguments for and against the use of statins are based around the idea of responsibility for one's own health.

? *If you were a family doctor, would you prescribe statins for patients with high blood cholesterol or would you ask them to change their lifestyle?*

? *Would it make any difference to your decision if the government had to pay the full cost of the drug?*

Who should pay for healthcare?

The key ethical question related to all these points is that if we make ourselves ill, should we be entitled to the same healthcare as someone who develops an illness through no fault of their own? At the moment healthcare does not look for a difference between natural illness and self-inflicted illness, but in the future people who continue to smoke or overeat may well find they have restricted access to treatment.

In the United Kingdom, all residents are treated for any illness or injury they may suffer, free of charge through the National Health Service. The cost of the NHS is met from taxes and payments made by those earning money. In the United States, the majority of people use insurance companies to pay for their healthcare. Many older people, those who cannot afford private insurance and those with handicaps are cared for through the government-funded Medicare scheme. Whatever the method of paying, much money is spent on self-inflicted illness and this takes away resources from other areas.

Affordable healthcare

Research costs, together with the need to produce a profit for shareholders, often mean that a new drug can be very expensive. Some recently discovered drugs that can help cancer sufferers and those with Alzheimer's disease may cost several thousand pounds for each year of treatment. High costs can prevent many patients from getting the drugs they need. In the United Kingdom, where the NHS meets most of the cost of drugs, it may be impossible to provide the drugs that are needed and, if the patient is paying, then only those with enough money will be able to afford the drug. The worry is that with the increasing cost of medical care in general, a 'two-tier' form of treatment will develop, with those unable to afford the latest therapy going without treatment.

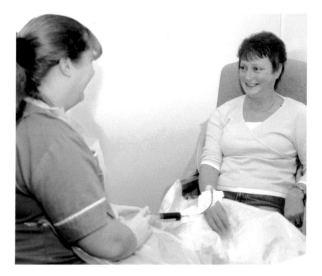

In several European countries healthcare is provided by the state, so people can be sure of good treatment. Elsewhere, private medical schemes are set up and not everyone can afford the best standards of care as a result.

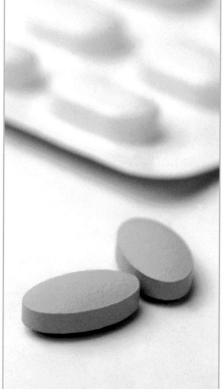

Statins are drugs given to lower cholesterol levels, and they normally have to be taken for life. By making lifestyle changes, though, people can reduce their own cholesterol levels without resorting to these drugs.

STATINS

Statin drugs are very effective for lowering cholesterol (a substance that blocks arteries and may cause heart attacks) levels and have few short-term side effects. The drugs are very expensive and patients are generally asked to take them for the rest of their lives, but can continue to eat a full range of foods. Another way to treat high cholesterol levels is for patients to change their lifestyle – take more exercise and eat less cream and fatty food – which costs nothing.

LIVING WITH HIV/AIDS

- *The estimated number of people living with HIV/AIDS in 2006 was 39.5 million.*
- *About five million South Africans carry HIV/AIDS – more than in any other country.*
- *More than 25 million people have died of HIV/AIDS since 1981.*
- *Africa has 12 million orphans from the disease.*
- *In developing countries 6.8 million people are in immediate need of life-saving HIV/AIDS drugs; of these, only 1.65 million are receiving the drugs.*

In African countries like Kenya, where HIV/AIDS is widespread, education programmes are being initiated to make the population more aware of the dangers of the disease.

Global healthcare initiatives

The developing world is also unable to afford the drugs it needs. HIV/AIDS is a growing problem in many parts of the developing world. The number of expensive drugs now available to treat the disease are unlikely to be available to people in these countries, who must look to less effective but cheaper treatments, or no treatment at all. The ethical issues involved in this problem are obvious – are doctors there to give whatever help is available to everybody, or just to provide treatment for the rich?

In the past, people never really gave a lot of thought to the suffering of those in the developing world. One reason is that communication was so poor that often they did not know what was happening. Nowadays, a disaster in any part of the world will be on our television sets and computers within minutes. This has led to a new moral dilemma – if we know about medical problems, is it right to do nothing about them? We may not be able to save every child who is ill but shouldn't we at least be trying?

Whose responsibility is it?

If the big problem is the cost of drugs, then should the developed world find a way of offsetting the cost so that people who cannot afford treatment are helped anyway?

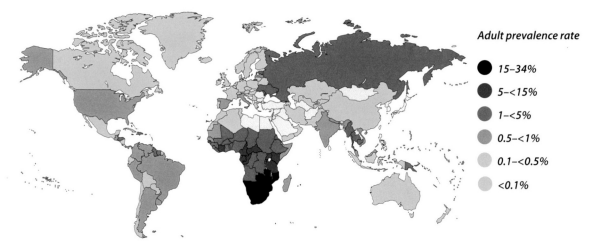

Adult prevalence rate

● 15–34%
● 5–<15%
● 1–<5%
● 0.5–<1%
● 0.1–<0.5%
● <0.1%

These are perhaps the biggest ethical issues of our time. Improved travel around the world means that diseases spread faster than ever – if the developing world is simply left with the problems of ill-health, how long will it be before those problems come to our doorstep? In particular, the problem of HIV/AIDS in Africa is not one that can be contained by that continent.

Doctors and other health workers can be found in every corner of the world that they are needed. The problems of death from simple infectious diseases and poor hygiene have disappeared from Europe and North America but still cause doctors problems in many parts of the world. It is all very well to try and apply ethics to medicine in our own surroundings, but do we have a duty to apply them whenever they are needed?

This map shows the prevalence of HIV/AIDS across the world. The worst-affected areas are parts of Africa. Should developed countries be doing more to help control and treat the disease in poorer regions like this?

" *Today, no walls can separate humanitarian or human rights crises in one part of the world from national security crises in another. What begins with the failure to uphold the dignity of one life all too often ends with a calamity for entire nations.* "

Kofi Annan
Secretary-General of the United Nations

YOU DECIDE

There is much debate about the role of the developed world in helping those in less developed countries with regards healthcare.

? *Are we in the developed world willing or able to share our resources with those in the developing world so that all can enjoy a basic level of healthcare?*

? *Is it really the responsibility of other countries to help, or should people be encouraged to find solutions to their own problems?*

 # Timeline

4th century BC
Hippocrates puts together the ethical code that becomes known as the Hippocratic Oath – still taken by doctors today.

1905
Eduard Zirm performs the first successful transplant of a human body part, transferring corneas from one patient to another.

1949
The World Medical Association formulates its International Code of Medical Ethics.

1954
The first kidney transplant is performed.

1956
The first successful bone-marrow transplant is carried out.

1957
The drug thalidomide is first given to pregnant women to control morning sickness. It is later proved to cause birth defects.

1967
The first heart transplant is performed in South Africa by Dr Christiaan Barnard.

1985
The Health Research Extension Act in the United States is passed to regulate animal testing.

1986
The European Union passes a directive to ensure that animal research is regulated in all EU countries.

1990
The Human Genome Project is begun, to decode the sequence of human DNA.

1992
The first liver xenotransplant is carried out. A pig liver is transplanted into a woman to keep her alive long enough for a human liver to become available.

1996
Dolly the sheep is born – the first organism to be cloned from adult cells.

1998
The first embryonic stem cells are isolated. Nineteen European nations sign a ban on human cloning.

2002
The German parliament votes to include animal protection in its constitution after pressure from animal-rights activists. It is the first country in the European Union to do so.

2004
South Korean scientists successfully clone a human embryo.

2005
The first full face transplant is performed.

2006
Trials in the United Kingdom of the drug TGN1412 go wrong and volunteers suffer damaging side-effects.

Further Information

● Books

Cells and Life Process by Denise Walker, Evans Brothers, 2006

The Discovery of DNA by Camilla de la Bédoyère, Evans Brothers, 2005

From Microscopes to Stem Cell Research: Discovering Regenerative Medicine
by Sally Morgan, Heinemann Library, 2006

Genetic Engineering by Steve Parker, Heinemann Library, 2005

Genetics by Anna Claybourne, Evans Brothers, 2006

The Human Body by Anna Claybourne, Evans Brothers, 2006

The Stem Cell Debate: The Ethics and Science Behind the Research
by Laura Black, Enslow Publishers, 2006

New Technology: Medical Technology by Robert Snedden, Evans Brothers, 2008

● Websites

www.biomedcentral.com/bmcmedethics An excellent website about medical ethics.

http://genome.wellcome.ac.uk/doc_WTD020902.html Find out more about the Human
Genome Project.

www.ornl.gov/sci/techresources/Human_Genome/elsi/cloning.shtml A website about
cloning techniques.

www.genetics-and-society.org/overview/quotes/advocates.html A website that examines
the ethical implications of genetic research.

http://stemcells.nih.gov All aspects of stem-cell research.

www.cff.org Find out more about cystic fibrosis.

www.nhlbi.nih.gov/health/dci/Diseases/Sca/SCA_WhatIs.html Details about
sickle-cell anaemia.

www.historylearningsite.co.uk/history_of_medicine.htm An excellent site on the history
of medicine.

www.uktransplant.org.uk/ukt/ More about transplant surgery.

www.newscientist.com/home.ns *New Scientist* online magazine.

www.sciam.com The website for *Scientific American*, the leading US magazine on science issues.

Glossary

Alzheimer's disease a disorder that affects short-term memory. Research has shown that the disease may have some genetic components, but it is not generally considered to be a genetic disorder.

antibiotics substances originally extracted from microscopic fungi. Antibiotics are used to treat bacterial diseases. The first antibiotic was penicillin.

antigen any substance that causes an antibody to be released by the body. Antibodies are a natural defence mechanism to combat disease.

blastocyst a ball of cells formed after the fertilisation of an egg; blastocysts are the source of embryonic stem cells.

cell the basic functioning unit of all living things. There are trillions of cells in the human body, and different types perform different functions. Cells contain chromosomes, which in turn contain genes, which determine specific features.

chromosome the part of the nucleus of a cell that holds the genes. Human cells have 46 chromosomes, and human egg and sperm cells each carry 23 chromosomes.

clone an organism that has been reproduced by cell division rather than by sexual reproduction. Cloning is generally the name given to the assisted process of forming a clone in an organism that would not naturally undergo this process.

cystic fibrosis a genetic disorder in which the digestive system and the lungs are affected. Cystic fibrosis can be diagnosed by a blood test given to newborn babies.

DNA (deoxyribonucleic acid) the chemical material that makes up genes. DNA is a large molecule that carries the genetic code to make proteins, which determine the characteristics of organisms.

double blind testing a method of testing drugs in which neither the patient nor the doctors know if a real drug or a harmless placebo is being administered. In this way any prejudice by the doctor or imagined side-effects by the patient are eliminated.

embryo the name given to the developing human in the first three months of pregnancy (see *foetus*).

embryonic stem cells stem cells taken from a blastocyst.

ethics a formalised set of rules generally developed from widely held morals. Ethical codes may become accepted by a whole society, when they often develop into laws (see *morals*).

foetus the name given to a developing human in the last six months of pregnancy. On birth the foetus becomes a baby (see *embryo*).

genes parts of chromosomes made up of DNA. Genes determine specific characteristics such as eye colour, skin colour etc.

genetic disorder a disease or disability that is passed on from one generation to the next through the genes. Cystic fibrosis and red-green colour-blindness are both genetic disorders.

genome the full set of genetic information that makes up an organism. Determining the genetic make-up of humans was the aim of the Human Genome Project.

haemophilia a genetic disorder linked to the X chromosome, in which blood does not clot properly. Females are carriers but males suffer from the disorder.

herbal remedies plant material used to treat diseases. Most herbal remedies have been in use for many years and have not been tested in the same ways as modern drugs.

HIV/AIDS the name given to infection with the human immunodeficiency virus. Some people just carry the virus while others develop the full disease.

infectious disease a disease that is spread by infection of the body by another organism. Bacteria, viruses and microscopic fungi are the main organisms involved in infection.

insulin a natural hormone that controls the amount of glucose in the blood. It is used to treat Type I diabetes. Insulin was once extracted from animal pancreases but nowadays most is produced from genetically modified bacteria.

In vitro fertilisation the fertilisation of an egg by a sperm outside the body.

morals a set of beliefs held by an individual. Morals may come from religious beliefs or the values of the individual (see *ethics*).

multicellular organism an organism that is made up of many specialised cells, as opposed to a unicellular organism, which is made of just one cell.

Parkinson's disease a disorder of the nervous system in which the body tremors and movement is affected.

placebo a harmless substance administered to half the patients in a double blind trial.

sickle-cell anaemia a genetic disorder affecting red blood cells, which gives them an elongated shape and reduces their ability to carry oxygen. This disorder is most common in people from Afro-Caribbean and Mediterranean heritage.

somatic stem cells stem cells taken from adult animals.

trial and error a method of testing something by trying one possible solution after another until one proves successful. While unscientific in nature, trial and error has provided the solution to many problems.

Xenotransplantation Transplanting organs or tissues from one organism to another.

Index

abortion 33
activists 15, 23
alcoholism 22, 38
Alzheimer's disease 39
animal testing 13, 14, 15, 19
antibiotics 13
assisted suicide 37

babies 26, 27, 28
Barnard, Christiaan 19
blastocyst 31
bone marrow 22, 33
Bush, George W. 33

cancer 15, 22, 30, 38, 39
cells 18, 22, 24, 25, 28, 30, 33
cholesterol 38, 39
chromosomes 24, 25
cloning 23, 27, 31
contraceptives 11
cystic fibrosis 25, 26, 27

developed countries 7, 11, 19
developing countries 7, 11, 40, 41
diabetes 13, 38
DNA 24, 25, 28, 29
Dolly the sheep 27
donor cards 20, 21
donors 18, 19, 20, 21, 22, 23, 31, 32
double-blind testing 16
drug trials
    animals 13–15
    humans 16–17
drugs 7, 8, 10, 11, 12–17, 25, 37,
    38, 39, 40

embryos 27, 31, 32, 33
enzymes 25
ethics committees 16
eugenics 28
Europe 7, 41
European Commission 27
euthanasia 37
exercise 7, 38, 39

fertility treatment 31
foetuses 26, 33
Food and Drug Administration 17
Foundation for Biomedical
    Research 13
Fox, Michael J. 33

genes 24, 25
genetic diseases 24, 25, 26, 27,
    28, 29
genetic engineering 24–29
genetic fingerprinting 28, 29
genetic screening 26, 27, 28
genetic testing 27
governments 6, 11, 15, 26

health insurance 29, 38
heart 18, 19, 20
    heart disease 38
herbal remedies 7, 12
Hippocrates 8, 9
Hippocratic Oath 8, 9, 11
HIV/AIDS 15, 38, 40, 41
Human Genome Project 24, 25, 28
hygiene 7, 41

immune system 19
in vitro fertilisation 31
institutional review boards 16
insulin 13, 25

kidneys 18, 19, 20

laws 10, 12
life-support 10, 37
liver 11, 18, 19, 20, 22
lungs 18, 19
lung disease 38

medical records 28
monkeys 13, 17

National Health Service 11, 38, 39

obesity 38
organs 13, 18, 19, 20, 21, 22, 23, 30
    shortages 22, 23

pancreas 18, 20
Parkinson's disease 32, 33
pharmaceutical companies 7, 11, 12
placebos 16
pregnancy 16, 22, 26
proteins 24

recipients (of organs) 19, 20, 22, 23
religion 10, 11
Research Defence Society 13

Secretary's Advisory Committee on
    Genetics, Health, and Society 29
sexually transmitted diseases 38
sickle-cell anaemia 25, 28
smoking 38
static encephalopathy 36
statins 38, 39
stem cells 30–35
    embryonic 31, 32
    somatic 32–33
surgery 6, 7, 18, 19, 20

Taylor, Amilia 33
TGN1412 17
thalidomide 16, 17
tissues 18, 19, 20, 23, 30, 33
transplants 11, 18–23, 33
trial and error 12

vaccination programmes 7
vegetarianism 11
volunteers 13, 14, 16, 17

waiting lists 22
World Health Organization 27

xenotransplantation 23

Zirm, Eduard 18